ENGLISH SKILLS

Comprehension

SIMON GREAVES

Series Editor

GRANT WALKER

Collins Educational

An Imprint of HarperCollins*Publishers*

Introduction

English Skills: Comprehension has been designed to help teachers deliver the English National Curriculum requirements regarding comprehension skills at KS2. It will also have extensive application at KS3. For those teaching in Scotland there is coverage of English Language 5-14 elements including "Reading for information" and "Reading to reflect on the writer's ideas and craft" to Level D. The content is set at an interest level likely to appeal to 9-14 year olds and at a reading level which should make it readily accessible to them.

The teaching of comprehension skills has, of course, never been separable from the delivery of English. Now, however the teaching of traditional skills such as developing a child's ability to express opinions about, reflect upon or be able to draw information from texts has been formalised in the English curriculum. There has probably never been more pressure on teachers to systematise the way they approach the teaching of comprehension.

English Skills: Comprehension covers curriculum areas under general headings such as Plot, Character, Style and Reflecting upon texts. Within these larger divisions, exercises then address specific topics such as language use, cohesion and structure. Detail of the coverage is set out in grids on pages 56 and 57. On the grids, which can be copied for record-keeping purposes, the major focus of each sheet is indicated by a grey box. Other areas which could easily be covered by the exercise are defined by a dark circle. Areas which might usefully be developed with extra teacher involvement are defined by white circles.

Each of the fifty-two exercises can be used to provide practice after a lesson, as a homework assignment, to provide a diagnostic assessment to establish what a child already knows, or to test what skills a child has acquired. Clearly, as with any teaching material, the teacher will present each exercise depending on circumstances. It is suggested, however, that the exercises be read through and discussed as stories before the questions are attempted.

Each exercise is presented as a complete, self-contained activity. They are presented in a variety of genre, including letter and recipe form, diary extracts and newspaper articles. There are also several poems, numerous original stories - some humorous, some more serious in tone -as well as adaptations of traditional tales.

Although self-contained, a number of the exercises are non-fiction based, relating to other curriculum areas such as history, art history, and science. It is therefore hoped that many exercises can be integrated into other schemes of work.

Whether fiction or non-fiction based, the material is imaginative, challenging and stimulating. The exercises are designed to develop a child's critical faculties and refine his or her ability to respond to a text in a reasoned, coherent way. It is also hoped they will be fun, helping stimulate imagination and writing skills.

A glossary of terms, some of which may be unfamiliar, has been included at the end of the book, together with answers to the exercises.

Published by Collins Educational
An imprint of HarperCollinsPublishers Ltd
77-85 Fulham Palace Road
Hammersmith
London   W6 8JB

© HarperCollinsPublishers Ltd 1996

First published 1996
Reprinted 1997

ISBN 0 0031 4397X

Drawings by Simon Greaves unless otherwise stated below. Corel Corporation: 6, 8, 13, 14, 19, 25, 32, 45, 49, 55. Image Club: 24, 29, 52. Totem: 51.

English Skills was designed by DP Press, Sevenoaks
Printed by Martins the Printers Ltd, Berwick

A Prelude book for Collins Educational

Contents

Introduction 2

Section 1: Plot
Cohesion
    The mouse and the lion 4
    The twins 5
Sequencing
    Scrambled egg 6
    Goldilocks and the three bears 7
    Penny Sangala, champion 8
Identifying the main idea
    School trip 9
    Kerplonk and Kersplatt 10
Identifying supporting ideas
    Soaps 11
    Staring into space 12
Extracting the plot/storyline from detail
    Sesi 13
    Aston oak 14
Extracting detail from text
    Sioux 15
    My dad 16
    Clouds 17
    Gem 18
    The sixties 19
Structure
    Rock solid 20
    Angus Macphee 21
Theme
    Cats 22
    Going up 23

Section 2: Character
Feelings: describing, reflecting, considering
    Dream house 24
    The Wallace collection 25
    Melissa 26
Emotion
    Crash landing 27
    Letter from Elizabeth 28
Actions: cause and effect
    If 29
    The diamond 30
    Storyboard 31

Section 3: Style
Description
    Aliens over Morpeth 32
    Time Traveller holidays 33

Atmosphere
    Notting Hill Carnival 34
    Macbeth 35
Interpretation
    The dark room 36
    Arnolfini 37
Tone
    The richest man in the world 38
    Fire drill 39
Mood
    Paintbox music 40
    On the beach 41
Language use
    A day in the life 42
    The magic bag 43

Section 4: Reflecting upon texts
Fact and opinion
    Henry VII 44
    Pirates 45
Bias and accuracy
    Cramer-on-Sea 46
    Vikings 47
Inference and deduction
    Camulodunum dig 48
    Computer game 49
Cause and effect
    Rain 50
    Skin! 51
Predicting
    Mystic Marge 52
    The clay pot 53
Identifying problems and solutions
    Etti's quest 54
    Sonu's problem 55
Content grids
    Pages 4-29 56
    Pages 30-55 57

Section 5: Teachers' notes and answers 58

The mouse and the lion

One day a mouse crept past a great, sleeping lion. Just as it was about to hide, the lion woke up and trapped the mouse by its tail. "Spare me, great sir! Spare me!" it squeaked, "If you let me go I will help you one day."

The great lion lazily considered the matter. It was amused by the boldness of the mouse. With a gentle swipe, the lion sent it on its way. They parted, and both the lion and the mouse forgot their meeting.

Months later, however, hunters were catching lions for a zoo in Europe. They snared the great lion in a net. Satisfied that it could not escape, they sat down for lunch.

Whilst they ate, the mouse happened to pass by. Seeing the situation, it quickly set about gnawing through the ropes of the net. In minutes the great lion was free. With a mighty roar of thanks, it bounded off. The mouse had returned its favour.

---

1   The mouse and the lion are both referred to as "it" in the story. Look at the lines below. Underline in the story where each line comes from.

2   In the space provided, write whether "it" refers to the mouse or the lion.

  A   "Spare me!" it squeaked. _____

  B   Just as it was about to hide. _____

  C   It bounded off. _____

  D   The lion sent it on its way. _____

  E   Satisfied that it could not escape. _____

  F   It was amused. _____

  G   It quickly set about gnawing. _____

The twins

Necip and Salmia were twins. Poor Necip was not well. He had a high temperature, his nose ran and he felt sick. He was a very miserable boy. Salmia, on the other hand was fine. At school she charged around the playground at break time, and played netball for her team against St Leonard's. She seemed a fit and healthy girl.

That evening though, she pushed away her supper.

"You odd child," said her mum. "It's your favourite. You must be unwell."

Poor Salmia was. She felt sick. She was a very miserable girl.

Necip, though, had been getting better and the next day he was back at school. He charged around the playground during break time and played football against Albury. He seemed a fit and healthy boy again. He was. That night he had about six helpings of everything for supper. "You greedy guts!" his mother said jokingly. "You'll eat us out of the house." She was pleased though. She knew he had recovered.

The next day Salmia was better as well. She and Necip both charged around the playground during break.

"You careless boy!" Mrs Wilson shouted, as Necip bumped into her for the tenth time. Then she blew her whistle at Salmia.

"Slow down," she called. "You're like an express train." Salmia slowed.

"The twins are better," Mrs Wilson said wearily, at the end of the day.

"It's great, isn't it?" replied Mr Day, the Head. "They've so much energy."

"Er, yes," said Mrs Wilson, sipping her tea politely.

---

1 Read through the story carefully, then list all of the ways in which Necip is referred to in the story, for example, Poor Necip.

2 List all of the ways in which Salmia is referred to, for example, a fit and healthy girl.

3 Imagine you are Mrs Wilson. Write her comment on the twins' behaviour for their end of term report.

4 Imagine you are Mr Day. Write his comments on the twins' behaviour.

These cooking instructions have been jumbled up. Rearrange the order so the instructions make sense. You may find the exercise easier if you first cut the sentences into strips.
What other steps could you add to the directions?

Scrambled egg

1   Place a frying pan on a low heat.

2   Pour the egg and milk mixture into the pan.

3   Add some milk to the eggs.

4   Add salt and pepper to the mixture, if required.

5   Serve on hot buttered toast.

6   Stir slowly. Do not overheat.

7   Beat the milk and eggs together with a fork.

8   Crack two eggs into a cup or beaker.

9   Remove the scrambled egg from the heat and allow it to thicken.

10   Melt a knob of butter or margarine into the pan.

11   Wash your hands.

English Skills: Comprehension © HarperCollins Publishers

Rearrange the order of these sentence groups so that the story makes sense. You may find the exercise easier if you first cut the sentence groups into strips.

Goldilocks and the three bears

1   While she was waiting, Goldilocks decided to use Baby Bear's video game.

2   One day they decided to go out for a drive in their new sports car.

3   Growing tired of this, she thought she'd listen to a CD.

4   "It's all right, it's only Goldilocks," Father Bear called. "She's over here asleep in my chair."

5   When she woke up, Goldilocks played with Baby Bear. After tea, Mrs Bear drove her home in the sports car.

6   Some time later the three bears arrived home.

7   Once upon a time three bears lived in a bungalow.

8   "Who's been playing with my video game?" Baby Bear cried.

9   The music was so peaceful and relaxing, Goldilocks fell asleep.

10   "Who's been listening to my CD?" Mrs Bear cried.

11   While they were out, Goldilocks arrived. She had come to play with Baby Bear.

12   Goldilocks found the bungalow empty, but being an old friend, she decided to wait.

Penny Sangala, champion

In this story, Penny Sangala talks about how she felt after winning the Junior World Championship in Gothenberg, and later injury problems.

Re-arrange the sentences so that the story makes sense. It may be easier if you first cut the sentences into strips.

1   To be honest, I can't remember much about the race itself.

2   A month later I injured my foot. It was terrible. There was this horrible snap in my heel, and a pain which shot everywhere.

3   I felt very tense before the final. I didn't want to let my family down.

4   Now I'm on the mend. I'm running again, but building up slowly.

5   Later I stood on the podium to receive my medal. There was a lump in my throat. I felt so proud, I couldn't stop a tear.

6   Waiting on the start line, my mind was completely clear and focused.

7   What I really remember was the split second after I'd broken the tape. I could hear the whole crowd going mad.

8   I want to be Olympic Champion. One day, I will be.

9   I was depressed for months afterwards. I had to hobble around with a heavy plaster on. I couldn't run of course, and I was really naggy.

10   Then Mum and Dad and the whole family and Ron, my coach, were crowding round me. I felt so happy, I thought I'd just float away.

11   I went through my warm-up routine, trying to settle my mind.

English Skills: Comprehension © HarperCollins*Publishers*

School trip

Feeldon Primary School is a village school in Herefordshire. It only has 68 pupils, and because of its small size, the whole school goes together on the annual school trip. This year the school went to Brodby Castle.

Read through the sentences below. Write an account of the outing for the local newspaper. Remember to include a headline. You are allowed to leave out any two of the sentences, but all of the remaining information must be included in some form or another in your report.

Before you start, decide which pieces of information are the most important and necessary to your report. Leave out the two pieces of information you think least important.

1 I was sick in the bus on the way home. I didn't mean to be.
Jodie Willis, Yr 1

2 Mr Jackson fell in the moat. *Aftab Gill, Yr 3*

3 An arrow went through a bit of wood 4cm thick. *Rosie Phipps, Yr6*

4 A falcon perched on my arm, on a thick glove. *Martin Pool, Yr4*

5 I was trying to point out some fish. *Mr Ian Jackson, Head teacher*

6 Brodby Castle is a magnificent, twelfth century fortified manor house. It includes a fine timbered Great Hall and Chapel. Brodby offers a morning falconry display and an afternoon archery demonstration on the front lawn. *Brodby Castle handbook*

7 We had to fill in a question sheet and do drawings. The infants had one of their own. *Arti Lal, Yr 5*

8 My sandwiches got all soggy. *Tim Boothby, Yr 2*

9 The children behaved very well. It was a long day for them.
Mrs Shirley Payne, teacher

Kerplonk and Kersplatt

Once upon a time there were two monsters called Kerplonk and Kersplatt. They had huge muscles, lots of hair and very small brains.

One day, Kerplonk began to dig a hole beside a high fence. At the same moment, Kersplatt began to dig a hole on the other side of the fence. The problem was that all of the soil and rocks dug out by Kersplatt sailed over the fence and landed in the hole being dug by Kerplonk.

At the same time, all of the soil and rocks being dug out by Kerplonk sailed over the fence and landed in the hole being dug by Kersplatt.

After many hours of furious digging, neither had managed to dig even a tiny hole. Confused, both paused to think about this for several seconds. Eventually, each decided to look over the fence. Kersplatt saw Kerplonk and Kerplonk saw Kersplatt.

After some minutes, both guessed what had happened but then carried on digging harder than before. Soil and rocks sailed over the fence yet neither Kerplonk nor Kersplatt managed to dig even a tiny hole.

This situation might have carried on for weeks, perhaps even for months or years, but one day a little bird flew down onto the fence ...

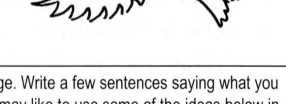

---

1 The story is written to give the reader a message. Write a few sentences saying what you think is the point, or message of the story. You may like to use some of the ideas below in your answer.

co-operation   **helping each other**   **thinking about things**

conflict   **trying new ideas**

2 Underline the words which are repeated most often in the story.

3 Finish the story. Where possible try and use some of the words you underlined above.

Soaps

1 ☐ I can't marry Greg. I thought Toby had drowned in a yachting accident. He survived it, but he lost his memory for two years... I've only just heard he's alive!

2 ☐ *Gran*:   My purse! Someone's stolen my purse!

   Rhoda: Calm down, Gran. You always think someone's stolen your purse. Look, it's on the table beside you.

3 ☐ Sharon thinks I don't want to take her to the disco, but that's not true! I just don't have a decent shirt to wear!

4 ☐ If you think you can run this coffee bar on your own, prove it!

Soap operas are very popular. Most are similar in that they tend to have lots of story lines, running together. Some of these will be important and serious, others more light-hearted.

Scenes constantly switch from one story line to another. Few scenes last for more than three or four minutes and some are much shorter.

Soaps almost always end on a "cliff-hanger". They leave the viewer wondering "what will happen now?" and wanting to see the next episode.

1 Study the lines of dialogue above. Decide whether each belongs to a main or supporting story line and write M (main) or S (supporting) in the box provided.

2 Using these lines of dialogue, produce a storyboard for one 30 minute soap. Think up its title and give details of setting, characters etc.

3 Write the dialogue for one short scene from your soap.

4 Produce a "soap survey". Do they fit the pattern described above?

5 What are the main differences between the early evening soaps and the later ones?

6 Which soaps are most popular in your class?

Staring into space

Our town is a scruffy straggle
of houses on the edge of a moor.
A thin hedge and a ricketty gate
separate the last house from
wilderness.

Passing the gate the other day,
I saw a man leaning against it,
staring into space.
He was young, in casual clothes
and trainers.
He wasn't doing anything,
just staring into space.
Two hours later, he was still there.

It worried me.
I mean, people don't just stare into
space for hours on end.
Not any more.
They might have in the old days,
before TV and fast cars
when there was nothing else to do.
Not now.
Not any more.

The man was there again, yesterday,
staring into space.
What does he think he is doing,
not doing anything?
Maybe he's got nothing better to do.
But why does he have to do nothing
there?
If he wants to stare at something all
day long,
why doesn't he stare at the telly
like everybody else?

Driving to work this morning,
I saw him again,
staring into space.
I wanted to stop the car
to ask him what he thought
he was doing.
But I was too busy.
I didn't have time.

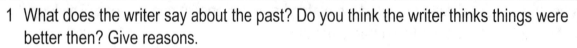

1 What does the writer say about the past? Do you think the writer thinks things were
   better then? Give reasons.

2 Why doesn't the writer stop and talk to the man?

3 Why does the writer think the man might be staring into space. Can you think of any
   other reasons?

4 In your own words, say what the writer feels about the man staring into space.
   Why does he or she feel like that?

English Skills: Comprehension © HarperCollins*Publishers*

Sesi

Sesi was late for school. Closing the door he began to hurry down the street. Hearing a loud noise behind him, he turned.

Sesi had the shock of his life. His house had blasted into space. It had taken off just like a rocket, and seemed to be heading for Mars. Sesi was alarmed, but then he saw his dad waving to him and smiling so he carried on.

Before long he felt the ground begin to shake. The next moment an earthquake opened up a crater all along Mallow Street. Sesi wasn't sure how to cross the crater, but looking down the street he saw a tree had fallen across the gap. He scrambled over it.

Hurrying along, Sesi heard a pounding noise above him. Looking up he saw four huge horses pulling the sun across the sky. Sesi wasn't too frightened because he'd read about mythology in school, but he was worried he was going to be late.

Heading towards Piltdown Road he saw it was cut off by a police road block. Sesi could see several people trying to catch two enormous lions. It would have been interesting to stay and watch, but Sesi cut down Wilson Street and got to school just as the bell was ringing.

The first piece of work Mrs Ireland gave them was part of their project on the environment. They all had to write about their journey to school. "She's never going to believe this," Sesi thought, beginning to write...

---

1 Although lots of things happen in the story, it is really only about one thing. What is the one main thing the story is about? Describe it in under ten words.

2 List the other things which happen in the story.

3 Describe two more things that could happen on Sesi's way to school.

Aston oak

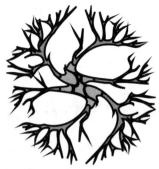

There is a very, very old oak near here but nobody knows exactly how old it is. Probably, when the tree was young, it would have been part of a great forest. Further back in history, most of Europe was covered in forest. The forests would have been home to wild boar, bear and wolves.

The first definite mention of the Aston Oak in history books is in an account of a battle fought between two barons in 1203. Troops supporting Philip de Mons gathered around it before the Battle of Aston.

By then the oak was a well-known landmark and must already have been a big tree. Most of the forest around the oak would have gone because the great forest trees were used for ship and house building, firewood and industry.

Originally, the village of Aston was situated about three kilometres from the tree, but the village moved. Like many other villages, old Aston village was deserted during the Black Death when whole families of people died. The new village then grew up around the tree, which still stands on the green. Over time, though, Aston has changed a lot. It is now a big town.

There isn't agreement about how long oaks can live. Some people think they can live for up to 2,000 years, others only 800-900 years. If this estimate is accurate, then the Aston oak is nearing its end. The tree is enormously wide but it doesn't produce many leaves. Oak trees get fatter rather than taller as they get older. Every spring, though, Aston oak seems to have new life. I wonder how much more it will live to see?

This piece of writing is about the famous Aston Oak. It is also about history, trees and forests, and about changes in Aston over the centuries.

1 In one colour, underline all sentences which are mainly about the Aston Oak.

2 In a second colour, underline all sentences about forests and trees in general.

English Skills: Comprehension © HarperCollins*Publishers*

Sioux

We do not live in houses. The world turns and we turn with it.

We follow the bison. We could not live without it. From its great skin we make our clothes and tepees. From its bones we make tools and from its horns we shape cups and spoons. More than this, the bison gives us fresh meat in the hunting season. Its dried meat feeds us through the long winter months.

Before the hard winter begins, we collect roots, potatoes, onions and turnips, then travel to our camping grounds.

We have few possessions. We do not own more than can easily be packed and carried. The earth provides all that we need.

When we camp, we place our tepees in a circle. This is because to us, the circle is a special shape. To us, life goes in circles. We are born weak, grow strong and become weak again in old age.

The seasons too, move in circles. Things are born and grow and die, but each winter is followed by a new spring. As winter dies and the ice and snows melt, we load our belongings and set off after the bison. We do not live in houses. We travel light. We take from the earth only what we need and nothing more.

When we move on, it is as though we have never been.

---

1 Make a list of all the things for which the Sioux needed bison.

2 Why did the Sioux need few possessions?

3 What shape was important to the Sioux? Why?

4 Imagine you are a nomad (somebody always travelling about). List your favourite things you could easily carry with you. List some of the things in your house you could not easily carry. Which would you miss most?

My dad

My dad is a clown. Yes, he is a real clown and he works in a circus.

Every clown has his or her own individual make-up and costume. This is what my dad looks like. Starting at the top, he wears a wig with a bald stripe down the middle. On one side of the bald stripe the hair has been dyed bright green, on the other it is red. Most of the time he paints his face yellow, though once, when he was feeling unwell, he painted it green. He paints a great purple circle around his left eye, and a great blue one around his right eye. He also paints a large black sausage around his mouth. His false nose is red, of course. It's long and lights up like a traffic light, but he won't tell me how it works because it's a trade secret.

He got Mum to make a special sort of jacket by sewing lots of arms all over it. At the end of each arm, Mum sewed a glove. Each arm and glove was then stuffed, so it looked solid and real. Dad calls it his coat of arms, which is a sort of joke - but not a very good one. He wears baggy, rainbow-striped trousers and huge, coloured shoes. He keeps all kinds of props hidden in his clothes; plastic fish, buckets of confetti, inflatable bananas and custard pies. In his right jacket button hole he wears a giant, pink carnation.

Oh, and I almost forgot to mention that round his neck he wears a huge wooden medal on a pale blue string. The circus master gave him the medal because he once did something incredibly brave, but he won't tell me what.

My dad's funny and brave, but when he's not being a clown he's quite quiet. I love him because he's my dad.

---

1 Read the story and then draw a picture of the clown. Use labels to name the things you know about from the story.

2 Then make a list of other things that you need to know to finish your picture, for example, how tall is the clown?

English Skills: Comprehension © HarperCollins*Publishers*

Clouds

There are three main types of cloud: cirrus, which are thin and wispy; cumulus, which tend to be large and puffy; and stratus, which generally form layers.

These names come from latin words. Cirrus means "curl of hair", cumulus means "heap" and stratus means "layer". "Nimbus" is another latin word. It means "carrying rain". A cumulo-nimbus cloud, therefore, is a heaped up cloud, carrying rain.

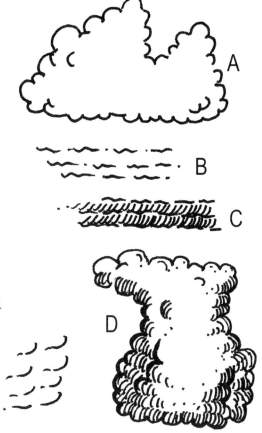

Definitions

1   .... a high, delicate, wispy cloud. Found at 9km. ( )

2   .... soft, fluffy, heaps of cloud. Generally found at 5km. ( )

3   .... low, flat, blanket like layers of cloud. At very low level it appears as fog. Found 1km or lower. ( )

4   .... mountainous heaps of thick cloud bringing stormy weather. Found from 3km up to 9km. ( )

5   .... thick, dark layers of cloud bringing rain or snow. Found at 1-2km. ( )

1 Complete the list of definitions by filling in the name of each cloud from the list.

2 Then match the picture of each cloud to its written description. Write the picture's letter in the brackets at the end of the definition.

3 Now draw a chart showing the height at which each cloud appears in the sky. Put the lowest lying clouds at the bottom of your chart and the highest clouds at the top.

Cloud names

cumulus, cirrus, stratus, nimbo-stratus, cumulo-nimbus

Gem

"It's all right, he's over here," Jamaine called to the others. "I can hear him barking in the bushes."

"Well, let's get him and go home," replied Billy. "I don't like it, it's getting dark and I think it's going to rain."

"I don't think it's going to be that easy," said Selessia, who was first over to the bushes.

All three scrambled under the bushes and peered into a dark pit. "I think we should go back for help," Billy said, "It could be dangerous."

"Well I think we should investigate first. After all, the hole might not be that deep," Selessia replied.

"I wouldn't care, anyway," Jamaine laughed. "I've always wanted to visit Australia."

Selessia looked into the hole and said, "It's not just a hole. It's lined with bricks and there seem to be metal steps down the side."

"Let's go for help." Billy pleaded.

From somewhere down in the hole they could hear Gem whimpering. "I am the oldest," Selessia said. "I think it would be safe for me just to try the first few steps."

"I'm bigger than you." Jamaine replied, "I should go."

"Well, if it's just a question of size, neither of us should go." Selessia and Jamaine both looked at Billy, but he turned shyly away.

Read the story carefully, then answer the questions.

1. Who seems to be the leader of the group? Give your reasons.
2. Who seems to be the joker of the three?
3. Which of the children was the shortest?
4. Do you think Billy was right to say they should get help? Give your reasons.
5. What do you think had happened before the story begins?
6. Write a story plan for the rest of the story.

  English Skills: Comprehension © HarperCollins*Publishers*

The sixties

The 1960s were a time of change. Change is not new, of course. Ideas, fashions and attitudes are changing all the time. What made the 1960s different, however, was the speed with which change happened.

One reason for this speed of change was the large number of young people in the population. These young people, known as the "baby boom" generation, or "baby boomers", helped spread new ideas.

There were also lots of jobs in the 1960s. The fact that there were so many jobs meant that young people could be independent. They had their own money and could spend it how they liked. Many spent it on clothes and records, and groups like the Beatles and the Rolling Stones became world famous.

Perhaps the most important change that took place in the 1960s was in the way women were expected to behave. Before then, most women had been expected to stay at home and obey their husbands. During the 1960s, however, women became more independent, and began to have more control over their lives.

It is important to remember that not everybody liked the changes. Some people think the 1960s "went too far" and would like to change things back. Whether you think the changes were good or not, they will be talked about for a long time.

---

1 The word "independent" is used twice in the writing above. Underline the two places it is used. What do you think the word means?

2 What name was given to the large numbers of young people?

3 List the changes you have seen in things like fashion and music.

4 List some important changes that have happened to you in the last three years.

Rock solid

I am a rock, old as the earth.
Wind and rain rage round me.
I am hard, yet
I know that I must change.

I am a stone, tide washed.
Other stones break over me.
I am hard, yet
I know that I must change.

I am a grain of sand.
Wind and rain lash me.
I am hard, yet
I know that I must change.

I am sunk beneath the sea.
Tonnes of mud weigh down on me.
I am hard, yet
I know that I must change.

I am rock once more.
Men dig me from the ground.
I am hard, yet
I know that I must change.

I am a statue.
I stand proud on a cathedral cliff.
I am hard, yet
I know that I must change.

I am weathered.
Acid rain eats into me.
I am hard, yet
I know that I must change.

I remain.
I watch the world change round me.
I am hard, yet
I know that all must change.

---

1 List the words and sentences which are repeated most often.

2 Which verse is different from all the others? In what way?

3 Of all the words you listed in answer to question 1, which do you think the most important to the poem? Why?

4 Write two new verses for the poem. For example, you could write about the earth pressures which forced the rock up from beneath the sea. Or you might like to write about the changes it saw as a statue on the cathedral, becoming surrounded by sky-scrapers etc.

5 Write at least one more verse to say what might happen to the statue. Remember to keep the pattern of words used in earlier verses.

 English Skills: Comprehension © HarperCollins*Publishers*

Angus Macphee

Angus Macphee didn't have birthdays like everybody else. For one thing, they were never on the same day. For another, he never knew about them until a twitching in his toes told him to walk over to a cupboard.

The cupboard contained 365 drawers, except in leap years, when there were 366. Tingling fingers would then tell Angus which drawer to open. For example, one year, when his toes began to twitch, Angus walked over to the cupboard where tingling fingers told him to open drawer number 68.

Inside the drawer was a birthday card and a little box. In the little box was an egg. Ten days later, a gryphon hatched out. Angus was very pleased.

He didn't think about his birthday again until the following year, which was a leap year, when his toes began to twitch. Walking over to the cupboard, a tingling in his fingers told him to open drawer number 179.

Inside it was a birthday card and a little box. In the little box was a piece of paper. On the paper were six numbers. He put the piece of paper in his pocket and forgot about it.

Three days later, on Saturday, his six numbers came up on the lottery. Angus didn't mind because he'd never heard of the lottery or that week's stupendous, triple roll over jackpot.

He carried on life with his gryphon and every year he was sent another wonderful present. He just never got any more prize winning numbers.

---

1 Underline all of the words and parts of sentences which are repeated most often.

2 Using the same pattern, write about two more of Angus' birthdays.

3 Assuming drawer no 1 is January 1, on what date did the gryphon hatch?

4 What was the date of the stupendous triple roll over?

Cats

Our cat is a purring machine
of smokey content.
Small, silky, soft grey,
sprawling, it lies all day in
pools of light.
When it yawns, its mouth
becomes a huge pink cave,
pointed with savage teeth.

Time passed. Africa
drowsed. Then
one sprang. An antelope
swerved and leapt
into the hunter's hungry jaws.
It was over.

There was a programme
on the telly about lions.
Two were out hunting.
Lazy, unconcerned, they
licked enormous paws
and squinted at the sun.
Nearby, two antelopes browsed.
Heads heavy, as if still half
asleep, the hunters crouched.

Our cat likes to lie beside
the gerbil cage.
It watches between half
closed eyes.
Waiting.
Waiting.
The gerbil twins
don't seem to mind.
All is quiet.

1 Which words describe what the poet's cat looks like?

2 Which words describe the lionesses?

3 What are the similarities between the cat and the lionesses?

4 What are the differences between the cat and the lionesses?

5 By comparing the cat to the lionesses, what is the writer saying about it? In what ways is it still a wild creature? Is the cat really peaceful and tame? Can nature be tamed?
    The poem's theme is about the extent to which humans can tame nature. Write at least a paragraph about this theme. Make sure you refer anything you say (about your own cat, for example) to the poem.

Going up

At the end of last summer
term, I was a bumble bee
playing the recorder.
Rachel and Heather were
bees as well.
We wore stripey jumpers
and black tights.
Our wings were made of
cardboard and our antennae
were bits of coat hanger
with woollen bobbles
bouncing on the end.
We were Y6 and it was
our last concert.
Some of the infants were
dressed as frogs.
They looked dead cute.

Mr Ross, our Head, made
a speech and wished us
all good luck.
I felt a bit sad.
It didn't seem that long since
I was in the infants.

I'm going up to the comp in
a few days.
It's like a factory full of
thousands of children,
all dressed in the same
dark, dull uniform.
I know I'm going to get lost.

Sometimes when I think
about going up
I get this tight feeling inside.
But I'm not really scared.
I know I can handle it.
Heather and Rachel are going up
too.
We'll be all right. We're ready.

On the surface this poem is about schools, but its theme is also about about growing up and friendship.

1 What things tell you the girl is writing about her primary school, in the first part of the poem?

2 Write down some words which describe the comprehensive.

3 What does the girl think about her new school? Write two paragraphs, one dealing with the child's thoughts and feelings about her old school and one about her new school.

Dream house

Last night I had a dream about a house. It was a very old house built of brick and stone. Plants grew up the walls and the paths outside were covered in moss.

In my dream, I explored all over the house. I remember thinking how quiet it was. I couldn't hear the noise of any traffic or TV or radio. It was as if the house was asleep. The only sounds I could hear were the creaking of stair or floorboard or the click as I closed a door.

The house was very old. I remember thinking about all of the people who had ever lived there. Lots of things must have happened in that house. Lots of people must have been happy at times, and lots unhappy.

One room felt very creepy. What had happened there? Was it haunted? The house didn't say. It kept its secrets. I sat on a stone bench in the garden and looked back at the house. Late afternoon sun warmed its red brick.

Then I woke up. I felt very sad. I wanted to visit the house again, and I knew I never could.

---

1 Circle the words you think best describe the house and its atmosphere.

spooky **quiet** **noisy** **peaceful** **modern** **busy** **old**

2 Make a list of all the facts the writer tells you about the house, for example, that it is made of brick and stone.

3 Make a list of all the things the writer feels about the house.

4 Describe a house you know well. Try and describe its atmosphere, what it feels like, as well as what it looks like.

The Wallace collection

Jean Wallace was a lost property manager. She worked for the railways and was very methodical. Everything that was found on any train had its place in her office, neatly arranged, waiting to be collected.

One day, Jean found something that did not have a place. It was a suitcase. She could tell straight away that this suitcase was different. You see, when Jean examined it, as she always did, she was sure she could hear seagulls calling to her from inside.

Now Jean was not a curious person, but even Jean was curious about this. Opening the suitcase, she had the shock of her life. For inside the suitcase was a real, wet ocean, and a desert island.

"Well I never," thought Jean. "Well I never."

The next moment she heard a sort of creaking and cracking noise. Looking up, she saw the suitcase had turned into a giant egg, and the egg was hatching. Out pecked a huge white bird. Stretching its mighty wings, it flew off over the station. Within seconds, it was completely out of sight.

"Well I never did," muttered Jean. "Whoever would have thought it?" With a gentle shake of her head, she went back to sorting umbrellas.

1　Circle the words which best describe Jean's character.

scatty　careful　imaginative　organised　excitable　neat　untidy

2　Circle the words which best describe Jean's reaction when she discovered what was in the suitcase.

shocked　pleased　unhappy　excited　amazed　curious　bored

3　Describe the person who left the suitcase on the train. What other luggage might he or she have had? Where was he/she going? Why?

Melissa

High up in a tower block, an elderly woman sat alone. The chair opposite her was empty, as it had been for the last ten years. "Melissa, Melissa! Come here!" a voice called. Melissa looked up. It was her gran. Grannie Simmons was standing in a dusty road. Her dark skin looked blacker still against the brilliant sky. The vision faded.

"I am a grannie now," Melissa thought. Beside her on a little table next to the telephone, were pictures of her grandchildren. The old woman thought back to her own school days in a low built shack with a corrugated roof. She had done well at school, her parents were so proud of their eldest daughter in her smart red tunic. Then she'd become a nurse. Somewhere in an album there was a picture of her smiling shyly beneath a starched white cap.

That was all before Wycliffe, and well before Britain. She thought of her husband, so clever, handsome and with such a good singing voice.

She thought of their arrival by steamship in Southampton. Everything had seemed so cold and grey. Times had been hard but she hadn't complained. Now her family was all doing well.

The phone beside her rang. It was Evangeline. "I feel very tired," Melissa told her daughter.

When they had finished speaking, Melissa made herself a cup of tea and went to bed. Then she dreamed of a sunny island far away.

1 What picture do you have of Melissa's childhood island?

2 In what ways was life different when she came to Britain?

3 List the things Melissa has been in her long life.

Crash landing

Egg Head in Shock Fall Drama!
"King's men useless!" blasts angry egg.

Wonderland was stunned yesterday by the news that popular local celebrity, Mr Humphrey "Humpty" Dumpty, had fallen from a high wall. Rescue services were on the scene within minutes, but it seems they were unable to put Mr Dumpty together again. The full story has been pieced together by ace reporter, Lewis Carroll.

The drama began at about 9.50 am. "I felt fine at first," a weak Mr Dumpty told me from his hospital bed. "Then suddenly I had this dizzy turn. The next thing I knew, I was falling through space."

"It was a horrible feeling, believe me," Mr Dumpty said. "If you're an egg sitting on a wall, the last thing you want to do is fall off."

"He landed with an eggstraordinary crash," one horrified eyewitness told me.

"It was a shattering experience for him," another reported.

"When I came round, I found I was surrounded by all the King's horses and all the King's men," an angry egg boiled. "They were worse than useless. I was very cracked up about it. My life was probably saved by the paramedics who arrived some time later. The hospital has been great. I feel comfortable. I am confident I will be back on my wall within months," Mr Dumpty said.

---

1 The newspaper article reports a range of emotion. Make a list of all the emotions and feelings it describes.

2 Invent some other headlines for this news story.

3 Write a newspaper report based on another fairy tale or nursery rhyme.

Letter from Elizabeth

5 Railway Terraces
West Crombie
Yorkshire YS3 2PH
2nd June

Dear Emily,

Thank you for your nice letter. I'm very glad you're all well. Of course I will help you with your project. Here are some notes.

The first thing to say about West Crombie is that I love the village deeply. Every house, shop and stick of fence has a story for me.

Things have changed since I was your age, of course. It makes me very sad when I think back to the old days. Although folk were poor, people seemed to have more time for each other then.

One big change was when the mine closed. I felt bitterly angry and extremely sad when it went. Closing the pit seemed like the end of the village. It wasn't, of course. In a way, I'm really proud of how we all coped. It shows we're still a community and that folk can still help one another.

Not that all was good about the past, though. For one thing, everything always seemed to be dirty.

The canals and buildings are cleaner now. That's important, because tourism is a big industry these days. We certainly need all the jobs tourism brings.

I love you all and miss you very much. I am sad you live so far away. I hope one day you will visit me.

Your loving gran,

Elizabeth

---

1   Emily's gran says she feels love, anger, sadness and pride. Write a couple of sentences about why she feels each of these emotions.

2   In what way has Crombie changed since Elizabeth was a girl?

If

1 On 31 August 1985, my dad overslept.

In his hurry to catch the bus to work,

....

2 He had to choose. If he went back for his lunch box ....

........................., but if he caught the bus ....

3 Deciding to go back for his lunch box, he ....

4 The bus was busy. So, because there was only one seat left, ...

....

5 After a while they began to chat, ...

....

6 My dad liked Mum so much, he caught the same bus again, ...

....

7 Next morning, my dad asked my mum out. ....

8 You can guess the rest. They fell in love, got married ....

....

9 You could say, if my dad hadn't forgotten his lunch box, ...

.... !

The words underlined in the story show the causes of things, the words which go in the blank spaces show their effect.

Read the story then finish each sentence using the list of effects below.

Effects

A   he would go hungry

B   and discovered they liked all the same things

C   he sat down next to my mum

D   he forgot his lunch box

E   I wouldn't be here

F   She said, "Yes."

G   he would be late

H   caught a later bus

I   and started a family

J   even though it made him late

The diamond

Two friends were exploring a new world. As they walked on, chatting in a happy way, the trees sprouted semi-precious stones and rare jewels.

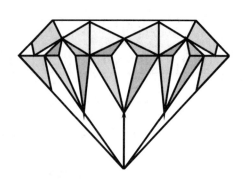

"How beautiful!" gasped Barbindar.

"It's wonderful!" Colin agreed. A huge, heavy diamond dropped at their feet.

Colin grabbed it. Barbindar tried to pull it away from him. They began to fight. Thorny brambles ripped Barbindar's leg. "Ouch!" she screamed. Colin ran off. Freeing herself from the brambles, Barbindar chased after him.

As they ran, the undergrowth became thicker. Rain began to fall.

Colin looked back and saw Barbindar was struggling. He didn't care. He ran on. Then the ground gave way beneath him. "Help!" he cried. He had fallen into a steep pit. In the dark, it seemed bottomless.

Barbindar heard his cries and smiled. The ground shook beneath her.

"Help me!" Colin called, slipping down the pit. There was something so frightened in his voice, Barbindar hurried over, despite her fears.

"You're all right!" she answered. "There is a path to your left." As she spoke the rain eased off. There was just enough light to direct him.

At last Colin made his way to the top. He and Barbindar hugged with relief. "Here," he said, handing her the diamond, "take it."

"Throw it away," she told him. Colin threw it into the gaping, dark pit. Hand in hand, they walked home.

---

1 Make a list of all of Colin and Barbindar's actions - the things they do and say. List the effects those actions have on themselves, each other, and their world.

2 How would you expect the world to be as they walked home?

3 What is the story trying to tell you about the effect actions have? Do you agree?

   English Skills: Comprehension © HarperCollins*Publishers*

Storyboard

Study the sequence of pictures. Two of the frames have been left empty.
   Fill in the missing parts of the story. You can do this either by drawing in the missing frames, or by writing a description of the action they should contain.

Continue the story as if you were a director creating a storyboard for a film or TV show. Do this by drawing frames in a strip. Show in a very simple way, what action is to happen in each frame. Add other instructions, for example, close up, music, fade out, etc.

Aliens over Morpeth

Three aliens hovered in their space craft about ten kilometres above Morpeth, in Northumberland. They were making a report.

The first alien, known as G2 was a tiny, round creature covered in trailing, silvery feelers. At the end of each feeler it had an eye and a nose.

The second creature, T3, was an enormous, multi-coloured, jelly-like blob. It oozed and sprawled everywhere. On board ship, T3 was kept in a clear perspex container, to prevent it messing up the flight deck.

The third creature was called ZZ20, though close friends called it Z. lts head was a great coil, whilst its body was long and thin, with a shiny metallic skin. Information ticked out of ZZ20's head on thin, foil-like streamers.

Each presented its report. G2 had been to a desert, T3 had been to the Antarctic and ZZ20 had studied the surface of a remote part of the Pacific Ocean. They had got hot, cold and wet. None had found life.

"Then we have wasted two minutes," G2 beeped. "There is nothing on this planet. Let us go. We have six more planets to investigate before tea."

In less time than it takes to read this sentence, they were sixty million kilometres away. Undisturbed, Morpeth continued its business.

1 Draw a picture of the three aliens.

2 Which words below describe the creatures. Draw a circle around words which describe G2, a triangle around words which describe T3 and a square around those for ZZ20. You may need to use a dictionary.

**furry   hard   globular   delicate   squidgy   peculiar   normal
large   gelatinous   sensitive   intelligent   linear   small**

3 Which part of the world had each visited? What problems might each have had, for example, with rust, freezing, etc.

4 What would they have found in your school? Write their report.

English Skills: Comprehension © HarperCollins*Publishers*

Time Traveller holidays

I was looking for a holiday with a difference, this year. Hearing about a little travel company called Time Travellers, I sent off for a brochure. When it arrived it looked like an ordinary holiday brochure, but flicking through, I found on page 12:

Dino World

Why not travel back 64 million years to the legendary time of the dinosaurs? For those seeking adventure and excitement, the Tyrannosaurus Safari Trail is a must!

The titanic tyrannosaurus, at 15m long with huge jaws and monster, 18cm teeth, is a truly terrifying spectacle! Not for the faint-hearted!

I looked at the cost of the holiday, gasped in disbelief, then turned the page. You could take holidays at any time in the past or future, in any part of the world. I glanced at a trip to Ancient Rome on page 23:

Our 14 day package includes five luxury nights in Rome, with tickets to the amazing Circus Maximus!

The tour also includes an exciting excursion to any part of the Empire of your choice. All hotels are modern, with hypocaust and hot spring baths.

I looked at the tour price. Then I fainted. "I think it's the caravan in Bournemouth again, dear," I said.

"Yes, dear," my husband agreed.

---

1 Choose four adjectives from the travel brochure, explaining what they mean. If you're not sure, check them in a dictionary.

2 Describe a Time Travellers holiday to your school or town. What are the attractions? Remember to use language which makes the holiday seem as interesting as possible.

3 From a magazine or TV choose an advertisement that you know well. What words and pictures do the advertisers use to sell the product? Do you think the product is as good as they say it is?

Notting Hill Carnival

Steel bands, reggae bands, rattling tin cans, everywhere you hear the rhythms of dance, the pulsing of life. It is a street party, pop concert, theatre and art show all rolled into one. It is the Notting Hill Carnival.

First held in 1965, the Notting Hill Carnival does things in a big way, writes Yusuf Shah. For a start, it is easily the biggest carnival in Europe. It lasts for two days, stretches along seven kilometres of streets in the Notting Hill area of London, and regularly attracts more than two million visitors. What's more, it's all free.

"The carnival is entirely organised by local people." Naomi Richards told me, "It is a community celebration." Celebration it is.

The carnival costumes have to be seen to be believed, extravagant, gaudy, bizarre, outlandish, fun. You name it, the costume is there. Some are vast, bright, swaying structures. Others look like gorgeous fantasy creatures.

"Carnival was started by black people," Naomi Richards pointed out, "but it is for all people. We want everyone to share in its fun."

1 Circle the words you think best describe the carnival's atmosphere. You may need to check some of them in a dictionary.

  vibrant   dull   exciting   noisy   boring   fun   friendly   tedious

2 Many of the costumes are so unusual, the writer had to use unusual words to describe them.
   Would you guess that **gaudy** means bright and colourful or dull and drab (cross out the unsuitable words)?
   Would you guess that **bizarre** means surprising and unusual or normal and commonplace (cross out the unsuitable words)?

3 List four important facts about the Notting Hill Carnival.

4 Describe an event, for example a big match or a party, you've taken part in. Try to give your reader a sense of its atmosphere.

English Skills: Comprehension © HarperCollins*Publishers*

Macbeth

Fog lay heavy on the moor. It hung in the leaves of the few, thin, ill-grown trees. It pressed against the hard, sharp boulders and stones. It swirled in the air, blotting out the feeble moon.

A sudden gust of wind ripped a raggedy hole in the fog screen. Three figures stood grouped in a pool of sickly moonlight. It seemed they had risen from the ground.

They were women. They looked as if they were waiting for something. In the distance a soldier's drum sounded. "A drum, a drum, Macbeth does come!" one of the women cackled. Slowly two figures emerged from the fog. They were Macbeth and his friend, Banquo. Behind them trailed a weary troop of soldiers.

"All hail Macbeth, next king of Scotland!" the women croaked. Macbeth turned pale and his twitching hands felt towards his dagger.

"What do you mean? Stop! Explain yourself!" he shouted. With a spine chilling laugh, the strange women disappeared.

This passage is based on a scene in a famous play called "Macbeth", by William Shakespeare.

1 Even at the beginning of the play, there are hints that Macbeth is planning to murder his king. The play makes Macbeth's world seem a cruel place. Find as many details as you can in the passage which suggest this, for example, the trees all seem to be thin and unhealthy.

2 The power of "Macbeth" depends partly on its atmosphere. There is a sense of darkness and evil everywhere. Do you think this scene would be as successful if it took place on a sunny beach? Give reasons.

3 In his play, Shakespeare describes the women as "witches" and the "weird sisters". What things are there in the passage to tell you that the women are supernatural, or at least, not normal?

The dark room

My friend Ann lives at 29 Maple Drive, or at least, she did. But it wasn't like other people's houses. For example, one time I went into the kitchen to find it had turned into a jungle. Yes, I mean a jungle.

The living room wasn't much better. Most of the time it was a mountain. Ann's mum and dad seemed to like it, though. They weren't like other people's parents, but then I suppose they wouldn't be, would they?

Only one room never changed. It was what Ann called the Dark Room. When you opened the door, you just looked into nothing. It's hard to explain. It was so dark and quiet and empty, it was like the universe must have been before the beginning of Time.

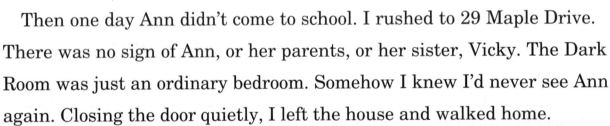

It was frightening, but it had a fascination. I could tell Ann was desperate to explore.

Then one day Ann didn't come to school. I rushed to 29 Maple Drive. There was no sign of Ann, or her parents, or her sister, Vicky. The Dark Room was just an ordinary bedroom. Somehow I knew I'd never see Ann again. Closing the door quietly, I left the house and walked home.

You could interpret (explain) this mystery in several ways. Tick which interpretation best fits the facts in the story, or write your own interpretation at D.

A ☐ Ann's family are aliens. They have returned to their planet.

B ☐ Ann's friend imagined it all. Nothing was ever odd about the house.

C ☐ Ann stepped into the Dark Room. Her family got lost looking for her.

D ☐ _____

_____

_____

Using evidence from the story, explain why your interpretation is correct and the others false.

English Skills: Comprehension © HarperCollins*Publishers*

Arnolfini

This picture is a copy of a famous painting by Jan van Eyck. It was painted in 1431. What is it about? Clues in the painting will help you interpret its meaning.

1 Study the picture, then tick the interpretation you think is the correct one, or write your own interpretation at D.

A ☐ The man is a detective. He has come to arrest the woman.

B ☐ The man and woman are getting married.

C ☐ The man is a magician. He is about to make the woman disappear.

D ☐ _____

_____

_____

2 Using evidence from the picture, say why you made the interpretation you did. For example, if you chose "A" you might say the dog is a sniffer police dog. If you chose "B" you might say the dog represents faithfulness in marriage, and if you chose "C" you might say the dog has just been pulled out of the woman's ear.

3 The man in the picture seems to be dominant (more important). Why? What things make him seem more important than the woman?

The richest man in the world

Four days ago I went to see the richest man in the world about parrots. You see, I run a charity which looks after unhappy parrots, and we needed money to repair cages and buy seed. Sir Percival had somehow heard of our problems and had invited me to call.

I have to say, Sir Percival was a surprise. He seemed a rather sad, shy man, but very kind. I found him writing cheques. Millions of them.

"Whatever are you doing?" I gasped. Sir Percival told me that he didn't like being rich and so had decided to give all his money away. He said I could help him if I liked, so I did.

I wrote out cheques to charities and Sir Percival signed them. Most of the money went to charities to help people in need or the environment, but there was still lots left over, even for funny little charities like mine.

Eventually, after non-stop writing for two solid days, all of the money had gone. We were both tired, but Sir Percival looked very happy.

"There's just one thing," I said. "What about your big house?"

"Your parrots can have it," he said. Then he left. I haven't seen him since, but I'm sure he's happy. So are the parrots, by the way.

Every piece of writing has its own tone. Sometimes the tone is serious, sometimes funny. Sometimes it can be a mixture of the two.

1 Do you think this story's tone is ☐ funny or ☐ serious? (tick which)

2 Do you think this story's message is ☐ funny or ☐ serious? (tick which)

3 In this story, the tone is achieved by exaggeration. Everything is larger than life, for example, Sir Percival is not just rich, he is the richest man in the world. Make a list of all the exaggerations in the story.

4 People say money can't make you happy. Do you agree? Give reasons.

5 Which sorts of charity would you give money away to? List five.

English Skills: Comprehension © HarperCollins*Publishers*

Fire drill

I was helping Mum cook yesterday. We were frying some bacon in the pan. I don't know what happened, but the fat caught fire. Then the fire alarm went off.

"There's a fire! There's a fire!" Mum shouted, leaping round the kitchen. She's under a lot of stress at the moment. The situation was serious but not nearly as bad as she thought. I turned the heat off and covered the pan with a fire blanket. The fire went out.

The alarm didn't stop though, and Bernie, Mum's partner, looked in. Mum was still leaping round the kitchen shouting, "Fire!" I suppose it was quite funny, but he shouldn't have laughed.

"Trying out a new dance?" he joked. Bernie's jokes are never that great. At that moment, Sandra came in. She's my big sister. "Oh, Mum," she said, all complaining. "You know it's not healthy to fry bacon. You're supposed to grill it. We did that at school."

Mum hit the roof. "Get out! Get out all of you!" she shouted. Bernie and Sandra left, but I didn't, of course. I made Mum a cup of tea.

"You're a good girl, Paula," she told me.

"I'm not good," I replied, "I'm totally brilliant!"

Mum smiled for the first time for ages.

1 Four people appear in this story. The tone of what each one says is made up by both the words they use and the way they say them. One may be sarcastic, the other serious.
   List the four characters. For each, write which tone fits what they say. You might write more than one thing for some characters. Choose from the list below. Add other words of your own.

   **serious   calm   hysterical   bored   whining   angry
           excited   insensitive   jokey   complaining**

2 What things do we learn about Paula?

3 Write this scene as a short play, adding stage directions and extra dialogue.

Paintbox music

If I could write blue music
It would be dark and deep music
It would be sad and slow music
It would be sea music.

If I could write red music
It would be hard and fast music
It would be sparky and hot music
It would be fire music.

If I could write green music
It would be lively and light music
It would be fresh and bright music
It would be spring music.

If I could write yellow music
It would be big and bold music
It would be loud and jolly music
It would be mid-day sun music.

If I could write grey music
It would be soft and gentle music
It would be cool and quiet music
It would be early dawn music.

If I could write you music
It would be red and blue music
It would be green and grey and
yellow music
But it wouldn't be you music
Only you can write you music.

This poem tries to give the poet's feelings about different colours - the "mood" they suggest to him. You don't have to agree! You might think grey music would be dull and heavy and lifeless. Or you might think red music would be dangerous and full of anger!

1 Write two verses of your own. They could either be about a new colour, or your ideas about any colour in the poem. Remember to set out your verses in the same way as in the poem.

In the last verse, the poet tries to describe somebody else, but says the only person who can write about you, is you.

2 Write a new last verse beginning, "If I could write me music..."
Choose words which say the most about you, for example, it might be happy or sad music, football or rounders music, lonely or party music. You decide - it's your music!

On the beach

"Over here! Over here!" I shout.

A frisbee arches through the air.

A dog barks. Excited,

we run to the sea and back

and back again.

I lie sunblocked, head shaded.

I cannot move.

I am a helpless, willing prisoner,

soaking in the heat.

I am free.

In a mad crazy dash into the
freezing waves

I leap into the crashing surf

pounded and pummelled

tossed and turned

I scream with raw delight.

Evening.

Our beach site is littered with

sunblock and half-eaten sandwiches,

damp, discarded towels and sand-

filled shoes.

Wearily we gather ourselves

and turn and trudge across the

foot pocked sand.

I look back at the sun sinking

into a flat calm sea.

Tired waves feebly break across

the shore.

1 Circle the words you think describe the mood of the first part of the poem. You may need to look up some of the words in a dictionary.

happy	**dull**	**depressed**
excited	**bored**	**angry**
	exuberant	

2 Write down two words which suggest the mood of each of the other three verses (or parts) of the poem.

3 The last verse begins with the word "Evening". Which parts of the day do you think the other verses fit?

4 In verse 3, the poet describes lots of action and excitement. Which words can you find most of, verbs, adjectives or nouns?

   What else do you notice about the words? Think about their length and sound. How do these words help create the sense of action and excitement?

   This verse only contains two full stops. Why do you think the poet has not used any more commas or full stops?

A day in the life

1 Glamorous TV star Cynthia Hemmingway brought traffic to a standstill when she opened a new superstore at the Riverside Retail Park. ☐

2 I couldn't see Cynthia Hemmingway very well because there was a big person standing in front of me. ☐

3 9.20   Radio Radsham, interview. Radsham.
   10.15   Springhill Superstore, opening. Radsham.
   2.00-6.00   Studio 5, rehearsals. Manchester.
   10.10   Amelia Springer chat show, live. London.
   11.30   Charity ball. London. ☐

4 All staff should be congratulated on the success of our opening. The presence of Ms Hemmingway ensured maximum coverage on local TV, radio and in the press. A wonderful beginning for us! ☐

5 I thought Cynthia looked really gorgeous. She had such a lovely smile. I thought she'd be taller, though. ☐

Springhill Superstore, Radsham, nr Manchester was opened by Ms Cynthia Hemmingway on August 5. Above are five extracts which describe the event. Each writer in the list below has a letter beside their name. Put the writer's letter in the box belonging to the piece you think they wrote.

A Ms Hemmingway's schedule, prepared for her by her personal assistant, Mandy Truebridge

B Eileen Bush, writing to her sister in New Zealand

C Anne Sullivan, journalist, writing in the Radsham Gazette

D Marcus Ford, Manager, writing in the staff newsletter

E Andrew Fisher, Yr 3, Radsham Primary, journal

August 5 was obviously a busy day for Ms Hemmingway. Imagine she had time to write in her diary when she got home from the Charity Ball. What sorts of things would it include about the day? What would the high and low points of the day be?

English Skills: Comprehension © HarperCollinsPublishers

The magic bag 1

Clouds hung over a town. One day, a vehicle arrived. The driver climbed out, looked around and sniffed with disgust. Then she searched in her vehicle.

At last she took out a bag. Opening it with a snap, she took out balls of colour. She threw one at a house. It was changed. It looked quite nice. Soon everybody was throwing them, at their houses and each other.

Leaving her bag, the woman got back into her vehicle and drove off, pulling the clouds behind her. She was never seen again.

The magic bag 2

Gloomy, grey clouds hung over a dismal, little town. One day, an astonishing vehicle arrived. The driver jumped out, looked around and snorted with disgust. Then she rummaged about in her mysterious vehicle.

At last she took out a small, battered bag. Opening it with a sharp snap, she extracted hundreds of glowing, glittering, many-coloured balls. She hurled one at a house. Instantly it was transformed. It looked wonderful. Soon everybody was throwing them, at their houses and each other.

Leaving her battered, bubbling, never emptying little bag, the woman jumped back into her vehicle and roared off, dragging the reluctant clouds behind her. She was never seen again.

The story above has been written twice. In the second version, adjectives have been added and verbs changed, but otherwise it is the same story.

1 Choose a sentence where adjectives have been added. What extra information do they give the reader?
2 Choose two of the verbs that have been altered. What more do they tell you about the woman?
3 Use a dictionary to check the meaning of words you are not sure about.

Henry VII

1   Henry Tudor was born in Pembroke Castle in 1457. ☐

2   Henry became King when he defeated Richard III at the Battle of Bosworth in 1485. ☐

3   His victory ended the Wars of the Roses. ☐

4   In 1486, Henry married Elizabeth of York. ☐

5   Henry was a greedy, cold, unfriendly man, who never smiled. ☐

6   Although he was not a nice person, Henry had a good brain and was probably the cleverest man ever to have been king. ☐

7   Henry was careful to appoint men like Edmund Dudley and Richard Empson. These were clever men who were good at helping him rule, even though they did not come from rich families. ☐

8   Henry VII was the best king England ever had because he gave the country peace and allowed farming and trade to grow strong. ☐

9   Henry was the worst king England ever had because he was greedy and was always taking money from people. ☐

10 Henry encouraged artists, musicians and builders. In 1503, his builders began work on a new chapel at Westminster Abbey. ☐

11 Henry VII's chapel at Westminster Abbey is part of the most beautiful building in England. ☐

12 Henry died in 1509. ☐

Read through the statements about King Henry VII.
    Decide which of them you think are fact (things which can be proved) and which opinion (a personal point of view). Put an "F" in the box if you think the statement is factual, an "O" if you think it is an opinion.

Pirates 1

Pirates are robbers who steal from people at sea. Many seas are not safe from pirates even today. Pirates were more common, however, in the Caribbean during the 1600s and 1700s. Pirates were attracted to the Caribbean because from there they could easily attack Spanish treasure ships sailing from the New World to Spain.

Pirates could be fierce and cruel. One of the most famous and feared pirates was the dreaded Blackbeard. A huge man, he sailed the Caribbean in the early 1700s and was killed in 1718. Not all pirates were men. Two of the most famous female pirates were Mary Read and Ann Bonny.

Many books and films have been produced about pirates. "Treasure Island" by R. L. Stevenson is probably the best known of all adventure stories about pirates. These books and films have not always been accurate. For example, it is unlikely pirates ever made anyone "walk the plank".

Pirates 2

Pirates are robbers who steal things from people at sea. Fortunately, piracy no longer exists, but it was a problem for the British in the 1800s.

Pirates were always men and could be fierce and cruel like the dreaded Blackbeard. They often made their enemies walk the plank. Two of the best known women pirates were Ann Bonny and Mary Read.

Most accurate information about pirates comes from novels, plays and films. "Treasure Island" by R. L. Stevenson is probably the best known of all adventure stories about pirates.

> The first passage above contains facts about pirates. The second contains a mixture of facts and inaccuracies. Read the first passage carefully, then go through passage two and cross out any part of a sentence containing an inaccuracy.

The way you understand the world and what happens will depend on many things such as your age, sex and where you live. These factors all influence what you think about things. This influence is called **bias**.

　　Below are seven statements about a summer holiday, and seven names. Read through the statements. Decide who is speaking, then write that person's name on the line at the end of each statement.

　　Write an account of the holiday from the point of view of one of the people involved.

Cramer-on-Sea

Alan Mugimbi, owner of Playland, indoor amusement park

Sarah Vaughan

Jess and Jed, Sarah's children

Michael Zimmerman, Sarah's partner

Sally Zimmerman, Michael's daughter

Steve Norris, ice cream seller

1 "The weather's been perfect for me. I've been busy all week. In fact, I've never done better." _____

2 "The weather's been terrible. Another week like this and I'll go out of business. I haven't sold a thing." _____

3 "I was sorry I couldn't fly my kite, but the Zap Game's been fantastic. I'd like to stay another week." _____

4 "Sarah's been great, at least she's joined in. Dad's too old. He's just stayed in the cafe." _____

5 "The weather's been appalling. We haven't even taken Jed's kite or the buckets and spades out of the car. I've done my best to keep them amused. I feel exhausted, I can't keep up." _____

6 "It's been all right. I didn't want to come anyway." _____

7 "I've spent my time in the cafe. It's not been too bad. I feel quite relaxed, really." _____

Vikings

A Ranghild, wife of Harald   **B** Brendon Lamefoot, slave

C Professor Olaf Petersson, Stockholm University

D Brother Anselm, monk   **E** Harald the Brave

☐ Discoveries this century have shown that the Vikings were excellent shipbuilders, magnificent sailors and great craftspeople, with a love of poetry and song. They also had their own parliaments in which all free men were allowed to vote.

☐ If I had a hundred heads and every head had a hundred tongues, I could not tell of all the misery the men from the north have worked. They have robbed us of our holy treasures. The Father Abbot is slain.

☐ I work the farm whilst Harald is away. Our land is poor. We could not survive without the wealth Harald brings back.

☐ I hate the northmen. They are wild and none fear death. I wish I was back home. It is cold here, and nothing grows.

☐ I am a farmer, not a warrior. I would rather plough the soil than fight but we are hungry. Our longship was paid for and built by the whole village. When we return the whole village will benefit.

---

1 Above are five statements about the Vikings, together with five names. Read through each statement. Decide who you think is speaking and write the letter of that person in the box in front of the statement.

2 On a separate sheet of paper, explain why each speaker takes the view they do.

3 Only monks wrote about the Viking raids. Give reasons why this might have influenced the way later people thought about the Vikings.

4 Draw a line down a sheet of paper. On one side make a list of all the good things about Vikings, on the other, all the bad.

Camulodunum dig

A recent archaeological dig in the old Roman capital city of Camulodunum (present day Colchester), yielded many interesting finds. These included:

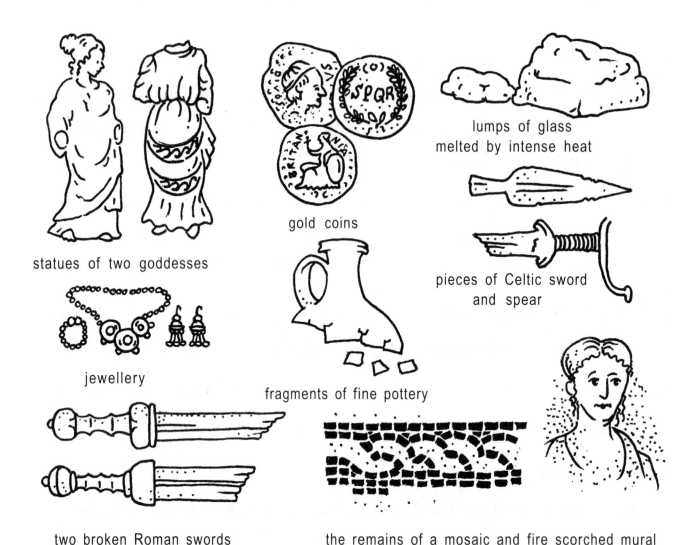

statues of two goddesses

gold coins

lumps of glass melted by intense heat

pieces of Celtic sword and spear

jewellery

fragments of fine pottery

two broken Roman swords

the remains of a mosaic and fire scorched mural

1 Study the objects found in the dig. Draw each one as accurately as you can, then write what each thing might tell you about the people who lived in the house. For example, the gold coins might tell you that the people who lived in the house were wealthy.

2 From all the evidence, what do you deduce (think) might have happened to the people and the house?

3 What other hypotheses (ideas, explanations) fit all the evidence?

4 Using reference material, learn what you can about Camulodunum. Was your deduction correct?

English Skills: Comprehension © HarperCollins*Publishers*

Computer game, a novel by Sarah Robinson

Extract 1 Back cover

It was supposed to be the greatest computer game ever. And it was. Until it became real! 300 thrilling pages. Read it, you'll never be the same again!

Extract 2 Chapter 2 page 12

The game flickered across the screen, sending out pulses of light and strange noises. The effects were brilliant.

Guy was playing, but five others were grouped around him. Muchun began to fiddle with some wires. Nobody seemed to pay him any attention. Guy paused, looked up from the game, and saw what Muchun was doing.

"Muchun, don't! Stop!" he cried. Alarmed, Janice turned round to see what was happening, and knocked Guy. His hand accidentally hit the "play" button.

Extract 3 Chapter 6 page 55

"Stop it, both of you! Arguing's not going to help any of us!" Muchun interrupted. "Let's all be quiet for a moment and think."

In the silence that followed, they could hear a building collapse. The sun died and they began to feel cold.

"I'm scared," Guy whispered, "I'm scared."

---

1 These extracts tell you only part of the story. Make a list of ten important facts you also need to know to complete your picture of the book, for example, how the characters escape from the game - if they escape from the game.

2 Imagine you have read the book. Using the information above and your list, write a review of it. Remember to include such information as a summary of the plot, the age of reader the book is intended for, what you liked or disliked about it, etc.

Rain

Rain is wet. Everybody knows that. But you probably won't know that even a small cloud can contain as much as 100 tonnes of water. The question is, how did it get there?

Well, to begin at the beginning, you really need to know that hot air rises. When you watch a fire burning you can see the smoke rise.

You also need to know that <u>when it is heated</u>, water becomes a vapour. Any time you boil a kettle, you can see water becoming vapour.

Finally, you need to know that warm air can carry more water vapour than cold air. When warm air meets cold air, condensation takes place. The vapour "condenses", turning back into droplets of water. In kitchens and bathrooms, because warm air from cooking and baths hits cold window panes, you will often see condensation on windows. As soon as warm air meets cold, droplets of water form.

So, to complete the picture, the sun heats water (in puddles, ponds and lakes etc.), creating water vapour. Then, because warm air rises, the vapour is carried into the air.

When warm air meets cold air, the vapour condenses into droplets, forming clouds. The drops fall as rain because they become too heavy. The rain forms puddles, ponds and lakes etc, and waits for the process to start again!

---

1 In one colour, underline all parts of the sentences above which contain causes (something which makes another thing happen). In a second colour, underline all of the effects (things which happen because of the causes).
    An example has been done for you. The cause is shown by a solid line. The effect is shown by a dotted line.

2 Draw a simple diagram which shows the process of vapour rising, condensing and falling as rain.

3 A word is used to describe the way water becomes vapour. Do you know what it is? If not, try to find out in your school or class library.

Skin!

Your skin is wonderful. It is tough and stretchy, but only 2mm thick.

It is made up of billions of tiny cells and is about ten cells deep. Skin protects your insides from dirt and infection, and helps control body temperature. <u>When you get too hot</u>, blood vessels in your skin open wider, letting more blood near the surface. This is why when you exercise you go red. The air cools the blood near the surface, helping you lose heat.

Sweating also helps you to cool down. When you're too hot, sweat is released through pores (tiny holes) in your skin. As this happens, the sweat cools down in the air, so helping your body to cool.

When the body is too cold, the muscles controlling hair tighten up. This makes your body hair stand up. In furry animals this is useful because air can become trapped between the standing hairs, helping to keep the animals warm. Unfortunately, it is not much use to hairless humans. We just get goose pimples!

When the sun is very strong, your body produces a dye called melanin. This makes your skin darker, helping protect it from the sun's harmful rays. People with dark skins have more protection from the sun. Whatever the colour of your skin, look after it. You need it!

Hair follicle

Skin

Sweat gland

1 In one colour, underline all of the sentences above which contain causes (something which makes another thing happen). In a second colour, underline all of the effects (things which happen because of the causes).
   One cause and effect has been done for you. The cause is shown by a solid line. The effect is shown by a dotted line. You will see that some effects can, in turn, become causes, making other things happen.

2 What should you do to prevent your skin getting sunburnt?

Mystic Marge

Walking around a fair, I saw a tent which said "Mystic Marge". I went in. Mystic Marge took my hand and looked at it for about ten minutes. Then she spoke, "You will _____," she said, in a cackly voice. I could have told her that, I was going home on the bus.

"I predict that one day you will play _____ for England," she told me. I don't know why, I've got two left feet. "I also predict that one day you will be _____." I tried hard not to laugh at that.

Mystic Marge stared at my hand for about another ten minutes. "I also predict that one day you will _____ tea on the dark side of the _____," she cackled. "Finally," she continued, "I predict that _____ and that _____ ."

I thanked her very much and left. It was raining outside.

"Bother!" said Mystic Marge behind me, "I've forgotten my umbrella."

"Why?" I asked, stepping back into the tent.

"Because I didn't expect it to rain!" she snapped. I hurried off, smiling.

---

1 Fill in the blank spaces from the list below. Complete Mystic Marge's last two predictions in your own words.

football	**beach**	**Queen**	**darts**	**King**	**sneeze**	**lawn**
travel	**laugh**	**Prime Minister**	**moon**	**chess**	**drink**	

2 List ten things you predict will certainly happen in the next week.

3 List ten things you would like to happen when you're grown up.

4 List ten ways you predict the world will be different in the year 2050.

The clay pot

There was once a great African king, called Atu. King Atu had many strong sons and a daughter, Etti. King Atu decided to set his sons a task. The son who completed the task successfully would one day be ruler, after him.

"My children," he said, "Far from here is a desert of burning sands. In the middle of the desert is a cave, guarded by fierce lions. In the cave is a small clay pot. In the pot you will find wisdom and courage and all of the other things a ruler needs to rule well. Whichever of you returns to me with those things, shall rule in my place when I am gone."

The brothers all wanted to be king, so one by one they set off. King Atu secretly hoped his eldest son, Ato, would win. Etti asked her father if she too could set out on the task, but he told her, "This is no task for a girl. You must stay here and look after your mother and me." Etti did not dare disobey.

From the sentences below, circle four sentences which could link together to finish the story? Write the four sentences in the correct order.

A   Ato crossed the desert.

B   Etti ruled for him during his sickness.

C   All the sons banded together.

D   Etti completed the task.

E   Ato returned home.

F   The king became unwell.

G   Etti saved her brothers.

H   The king changed his mind.

I   The sons all got into difficulty.

J   Ato tricked the lions.

K   The sons helped each other across the desert and past the lions.

L   Etti stayed at home.

M   The king decided Etti would be the best ruler.

N   The sons all voted to choose the next leader.

O   Etti set out on her task.

P   Ato became king.

Etti's quest

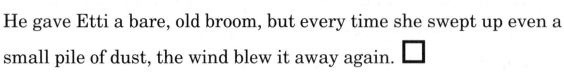

1 The bandit king threw Etti into a deep, dark pit. Its walls were steep and smooth. She could not climb them. ☐

2 "You must sweep my courtyard clean of every speck of dust," the farmer said, "otherwise I will keep you here to be my wife." He gave Etti a bare, old broom, but every time she swept up even a small pile of dust, the wind blew it away again. ☐

3 Etti was surrounded by trees and vegetation. As soon as she pushed one branch or leaf aside, another sprang up. She was trapped. ☐

4 The desert burned before her. She knew she would have to cross it, if she were to complete her quest. ☐

Princess Etti, is on a quest. On it she makes many friends but faces many dangers. Above is a list of the problems she faces, below is a list of solutions. Match them up by writing each solution's letter in the box provided after the problem. You can only use a letter once.

A   She stared as an army of termites munched their way towards her. They ate everything in their path. Within minutes, the way was clear.

B   Etti had never seen so many ants. Every ant carried away one speck.

C   She unrolled the mat given her by the wise old woman. Etti stepped on and sat down. The mat carried her gently but swiftly through the air.

D   The spiders quickly agreed to spin their threads together. Within an hour they had spun a thick rope, which they lowered down.

These episodes in Etti's story leave out much detail. For example, they do not tell you how she met the wise old woman or why she was thrown in a pit. Nor do they tell you how Etti made friends with the creatures who came to her rescue. Write a story plan for one of the episodes, filling in the missing details. Remember, you do not have to write the whole story, just its outline.

Sonu's problem

Sonu Swaminathan was a wanted man. He was a very wanted man. That was his problem. Sonu was desperately needed by his local football team, Traversham United. He was their captain, leading goal scorer, and easily the team's best player.

With Sonu's help, Traversham had won their way through to the Farrow League Cup Final. The match was to be played on Sat 22 May.

On the same weekend, however, Sonu had been invited to take part in an Initiative Training Course. Sonu worked for Darrant International, and the company had spotted his leadership potential.

Sonu was confused. On the one hand, he did not want to let his team down. He knew his friends depended on him. On the other hand, the business course was a fast track to promotion. By the age of twenty five he could be running a Darrant company anywhere in the world. He found that prospect exciting.

Sonu wondered if he could join the course half way through, after the match. He was worried though, that if Darrant thought he wasn't really keen, they wouldn't be interested in him.

When he eventually told his mum about the problem she burst out laughing. "No wonder they want to send you on an Initiative Training Course," she joked. "The answer is simple."

So what is it?

---

1 Do you think "using initiative" means:

         sticking to the rules   or   *taking imaginative, independent action*?

   Cross out the wrong definition.

2 Does your school give you opportunities to use your initiative?

3 Make a list of all the reasons for Sonu to play in the cup final. Then make a list of all the reasons to go on the training weekend.

4 How would you solve Sonu's problem?

Legend:
- ■ Major focus of sheet
- ● Other coverage
- ○ Could be developed by teacher

Page	Story title	Fiction	Non-fiction	Cohesion	Sequencing	Identifying the main idea	Identifying supporting ideas	Extracting the plot/storyline	Extracting detail from text	Structure	Theme	Feelings	Emotion	Actions: cause and effect	Description	Atmosphere	Interpretation	Tone	Mood	Language use	Fact and opinion	Bias and accuracy	Inference and deduction	Cause and effect	Predicting	Problems and solutions
4	The mouse and the lion	●		■		●			●					●				●								○
5	The twins	●		■						●												●				
6	Scrambled egg		●		■															●						
7	Goldilocks	●		○	■									○				○	○	●						
8	Penny Sangala, champion		●	○	■									○		○		●		●						
9	School trip	●				■		●				●	●										●			
10	Kerplonk and Kersplatt	●		○		■				●		○	○	●	●			●		●		●			●	●
11	Soaps	●				●			●			●	○	●						●					●	○
12	Staring into space	●		○		●		○	●			●		●	●	○	●		○	●						
13	Sesi			○			■	■												○						
14	Aston oak		●	○			■	■				●			○			●			○			●		
15	Sioux	●		○			●		■			○			●					●	○					
16	My dad		●	○		●			■			●			●			●		●						
17	Clouds		●			●			■			●	●		●											
18	Gem		●						■				●	●				○		○	○			○	●	●
19	The sixties	●							■		●									●	○			●		
20	Rock solid	●		○		●	●		●	■				●										●		
21	Angus Macphee		●			●			●	■								●		●		●	●			
22	Cats	●		○		●	○		●		■	■	○	○	●		●	○	●	●						
23	Going up	●				●	●		●		■				●			○	○	○						
24	Dream house	●		○		●	●		●			■	○	○	●	●		○		○						
25	The Wallace collection	●				○			●			■	○					●								○
26	Melissa	●							●			■			●		●	●	●	●						
27	Crash landing	●		○					●				■	○				●				○				
28	Letter from Elizabeth		●						●				■					●			○					
29	If	●		○					●			○	○	■												●

Key:

- ■ = Major focus of sheet
- ● = Other coverage
- ○ = Could be developed by teacher

Column abbreviations: Fic = Fiction · NonFic = Non-fiction · Coh = Cohesion · Seq = Sequencing · Main = Identifying the main idea · Supp = Identifying supporting ideas · Plot = Extracting the plot/storyline · Detail = Extracting detail from text · Struct = Structure · Theme = Theme · Feel = Feelings · Emot = Emotion · ActCE = Actions: cause and effect · Descr = Description · Atmos = Atmosphere · Interp = Interpretation · Tone = Tone · Mood = Mood · Lang = Language use · FactOp = Fact and opinion · Bias = Bias and accuracy · Inf = Inference and deduction · CauseEff = Cause and effect · Pred = Predicting · Prob = Problems and solutions

Page	Story title	Fic	NonFic	Coh	Seq	Main	Supp	Plot	Detail	Struct	Theme	Feel	Emot	ActCE	Descr	Atmos	Interp	Tone	Mood	Lang	FactOp	Bias	Inf	CauseEff	Pred	Prob
30	The diamond	●		○		●			●	●		●	●	■	●		●			●					●	○
31	Storyboard	●		○								●		■											●	●
32	Aliens over Morpeth	●		○					●						■								○			
33	Time Traveller holidays	●	●	○											■											
34	Notting Hill Carnival		●	○					●				●		●	■		●		●	○	○				
35	Macbeth	●		○					●			●	○		●	■		○		●						
36	The dark room	●							●				○		●		■	○		●			●			
37	Arnolfini		●			●						○		○	●		■									
38	The richest man in the world		●			●			●			○		○				■			○					○
39	Fire drill	●		○						●		●	●	●				■								○
40	Paintbox music	●		○		○						●	○													
41	On the beach	●				○						●	○							●						
42	A day in the life	●		○					●			●	●						■							
43	The magic bag	●						○				●		●	●	○	●		■			●	○			○
44	Henry VII		●			○															■					
45	Pirates		●	○					●					○						■	■	●				
46	Cramer-on-Sea		●	○		●			●											■		■				●
47	Vikings		●	○		●			●												●	■				
48	Camulodunum dig		●	○		●	●					●	●	●	○		●		○				■			●
49	Computer game	●		○		●	○					●	●	●	○	○	●	○	○	○	●		■			
50	Rain		●	○					●			○	●						○	○	○			■		
51	Skin!		●	○					●											○				■		
52	Mystic Marge	●										○													■	
53	The clay pot	●		○		●		○		○				●											■	●
54	Etti's quest	●								●		○		●									●			■
55	Sonu's problem	●							○			●	○	●							○					■

Teachers' notes and answers

Cohesion: pages 4 & 5

Even simple texts require the reader to carry concepts or notions from one sentence to the next, for example:

> *The ball is soft and blue. Anil is playing with it.*

Here, the reader has to identify that the pronoun in the second sentence relates back to the ball. Without that grasp, the second sentence can have no meaning. That being able to link a part to the whole or see how one word or idea links back to another, represents cohesion.

Answers
The mouse and the lion
1 A paragraph 1 ● B paragraph 1 ● C paragraph 4 ● D paragraph 2 ● E paragraph 3 ● F paragraph 2 ● G paragraph 4
2 A mouse ● B mouse ● C lion ● D mouse ● E lion ● F lion ● G mouse

The twins
1 Poor Necip ● very miserable boy ● fit and healthy boy ● greedy guts ● careless boy
2 fine ● fit and healthy girl ● odd child ● Poor Salmia ● a very miserable girl ● better ● like an express train
3 Open ended but Mrs Wilson's report should stress the need for more control and self-discipline.
4 Mr Day's might mention the great contribution their energy makes to the school teams.

Sequencing: pages 6 to 8

To a degree, any sequencing activity must involve elements of cohesion, and may involve structure. Essentially, a sequencing exercise requires a child or group to re-order a jumbled collection of sentences, pictures etc. so they form a coherent whole.

In some instances, the re-ordering may be subjective but in others must follow a definite sequence.

It is a valuable exercise because it requires a child to focus on a work's structure, correctly identifying how one part of the whole relates to another. As a group activity, sequencing can be as valuable since it may stimulate discussion about the most logical ordering of the sentences in hand.

Answers
Scrambled egg
One logical sequence is: 11, 8, 3, 7, 4, 1, 10, 2, 6, 9, 5

Goldilocks and the three bears
One sequence is: 7, 2, 11, 12, 1, 3, 9, 6, 8, 10, 4, 5

Penny Sangala, champion
One sequence is: 3, 11, 6, 1, 7, 10, 5, 2, 9, 4, 8

Identifying the main idea: pages 9 & 10

One of the most obvious ways to focus a child's attention on the main idea of a story, is through the genre of a fable with a clear moral (e.g. Aesop's fable). Although an original story, *Kerplonk and Kersplatt* follows this pattern.

The school trip adopts a different approach, requiring the pupil to sift evidence. A first requirement of this exercise is to discard the least relevant information, the next to organise the material, giving greatest attention to the most significant detail.

Answers
School trip
The two least important pieces of information are probably 1 and 8.

Kerplonk and Kersplatt
1 No set response.
2 The repeated words include: dig, fence, soil, rocks, sailed, over, hole.
3 No set response.

Identifying supporting ideas: pages 11 & 12

Any complex text will convey information of varying importance to the reader. *Soaps* and *Staring into space* are both exercises which ask the pupil to analyse the information in the text, separating their important ideas from subsidiary ones.

Answers
Soaps
1 1 M ● 2 S ● 3 S ● 4 M
2-6 No set response.

Staring into space
1 The past was boring, no TV or fast cars, nothing else to do.
2 Too busy, no time to stop.
3 Man has nothing better to do. Other reasons might include: looking at greenery, bird watching, thinking, feeling sad.
4 Writer is uncomfortable/irritated/annoyed/mystified. The man's silence and peace clashes with the writer's hurried modern life.

Extracting the plot/storyline from detail: pages 13 & 14

The essence of a plot can be extremely simple, but may be missed when overlaid or complicated by secondary plots. The plot of Homer's *Odyssey*, for example, is the story of Ulysses' return from Troy.

His adventures on the way home are subordinate to the essential story of his return. *Sesi* was inspired by Homer's epic!

Answers

Sesi

1 Story is about Sesi's journey to school.
2 House blasts into space ● Earthquake ● Horses pull sun across sky ● Lions being captured.
3 No set response.

Aston oak

1 About Aston Oak: There is ... it is. ● Probably, when ... great forest. ● The first ... in 1203. ● Troops supporting ... of Aston. ● By then ... big tree. ● The new ... the green. ● If this ... its end. ● The tree ... many leaves. ● Every spring ... new life.
2 About forests and trees: Further back ... in forest. ● The forests ... and wolves. ● Most of ... and industry. ● There isn't ... can live. ● Some people ... 800-900 years. ● Oak trees ... get older.

Extracting detail from text: pages 15 to 19

In a sense, all comprehension centred activities are based on extracting detail from text. Without the ability to analyse a text (whether telephone book or Shakespeare), and take from it the desired information, a text becomes little more than meaningless strings of words.

These exercises require a variety of responses.

Answers

Sioux

1 Sioux needed bison for clothes, tepees, tools, cups, spoons, fresh meat, dried meat.
2 They needed few possessions because the earth provided for them, they lived off the land.
3 The circle was important because seasons and life go in circles.
4 No set response.

My dad

1 Drawing and labels might include: wig with bald stripe, bright green hair, red hair, yellow face, purple circle around left eye, blue circle around right eye, black sausage around mouth, red nose, light in nose, jacket with lots of arms, stuffed glove at end of each arm, baggy, rainbow-striped trousers, huge, coloured shoes, plastic fish, buckets of confetti, inflatable bananas, custard pies, giant, pink carnation, huge wooden medal around neck, pale blue string.
2 No set response.

Clouds

1 1 cirrus ● 2 cumulus ● 3 stratus ● 4 cumulo-nimbus ● 5 nimbo-stratus
2 1 E ● 2 A ● 3 B ● 4 D ● 5 C
3 Chart would look something like:

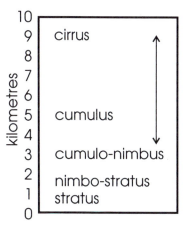

Gem

1 Selessia: first to bushes, suggests investigating, is the oldest, is positive and assertive.
2 Jamaine
3 Selessia
4-6 No set response.

The sixties

1 Independent appears in paragraphs 3 (line 3) and 4 (line 5)
2 Baby boom generation/baby boomers

Structure: pages 20 & 21

Almost any text will have a definable structure - a beginning, middle and end, for example. Within that structure, there may be additional structures such as repetitions of phrase or recurring motifs. These internal, shaping structures, help give the text, whether poem, rhyme or story, a strength and rhythm. Structures are more easily identified in traditional tales such as "The three little pigs" or "Rumplestiltskin" or rhymes and songs such as "There was an old lady who swallowed a fly" or "Old MacDonald".

The strong repetitions involved in these examples variously lend humour, tension or pacing to the story or rhyme. In every case, they also encourage a younger child's involvement, allowing him or her the confidence of anticipation (as a familiar sentence begins) but also the pleasure of surprise (as a new twist is introduced). Such repetitions also help the beginning reader gain confidence as familiar words and phrases recur.

In an older, more sophisticated reader, the ability to identify structures within a text will naturally lead into his or her being able to identify more subtle, underlying aspects of the work such as themes or recurrent imagery.

Answers

Rock solid

1 I ● am ● me ● wind ● rain ● I am hard yet ● I know that I must change
2 Final verse is different, first line begins "I

remain", not "I am", last line is "I know that *all* must change".

3 Most important word is "change".

4 No set response.

Angus Macphee

1 twitching • cupboard • tingling fingers • toes began to twitch • drawer • birthday card • little box

2 No set response.

3 March 19

4 June 27 (leap year)

Theme: pages 22 & 23

If the plot of any work is about how "a" relates to "b" and "c" - the mechanics of the action - then the theme tells you "what" that action signifies. For example, the plot of *Cats* describes a domestic cat and two lionesses hunting in their different ways. The poem's theme is about the extent to which nature can be tamed. The domestic cat shares a human environment (as do the gerbils), but its instincts remain wild.

Answers
Cats

1 Cat: purring machine • smokey • small • silky • soft grey • sprawling • mouth is huge pink cave • savage teeth

2 Lionesses: lazy • unconcerned • enormous paws • squinting • heads heavy as if still asleep • crouched

3 Similarities: both are patient, lazy, watchful. Lioness squints, cat has half closed eyes.

4 Differences: Cat is small and silky whilst lionesses are enormous, heavy. Cat is domesticated and its prey is unobtainable, lionesses are wild and are safely seen on TV.

5 No set response.

Going up

1 Children were Y6 • some children were "infants".

2 Factory • thousands of children • dark, dull uniforms • bewildering

3 No set response.

Feelings: describing, reflecting, considering: pages 24 to 26

As defined for these exercises, "feelings" are distinguished from emotion only by degree. Necessarily, emotions are feelings. "Emotion" is used to mean the larger, more demonstrative range of expression. In these exercises, "feelings" are associated with a more subtle, quieter response to experience

Answers
Dream house

1 spooky quiet peaceful old

2 very old • built of brick and stone • plants grew up walls • paths covered in moss • creaking stairs or floorboard • stone bench • garden • red brick

3 quiet • house was asleep • people must have been happy and unhappy • one room felt creepy • secretive • sadness

4 No set response.

The Wallace collection

1 careful • organised • neat

2 curious • shocked • amazed

3 No set response.

Melissa

1 Island was hot • brilliant skies • dusty roads • sunny • happy • palm trees (using picture for further information)

2 It was cold • grey • times were hard

3 Melissa had been: widow, wife, child, eldest daughter, granddaughter, grannie, old woman, student, nurse, mother, migrant

Emotion: pages 27 & 28

Answers
Crash landing

1 stunned • weak • felt fine • horrible feeling • horrified • shattering • angry • boiled • cracked up • feel comfortable • confident

2 & 3 No set response.

Letter from Elizabeth

1 Love of village because she knows it so well • anger at closing of mine with consequences for everyone • sadness at possible demise of village • pride at how village coped, everyone helping

2 People have less time for each other • mines have closed • things are cleaner • tourism has replaced mining

Actions: cause and effect: pages 29 to 31

According to Newton, every action has an equal and opposite reaction. In the first set of exercises, causes and effects are largely the product of human initiative - the effect not always calculable.

In the second, the exercises explore more deterministic, "natural" sequences of cause and effect.

Answers
If

1 D • 2 G, A • 3 H • 4 C • 5 B • 6 J • 7 F • 8 I • 9 E

The diamond

Note that answers to this exercise can be at either a simple or a complex level.

A=Action E=Effect

A Two friends were exploring a new world. As they walked on, chatting in a happy way

E trees sprouted semi-precious stones and rare jewels

A "How beautiful!" gasped Barbindar. "It's wonderful!" Colin agreed.

E A huge, heavy diamond dropped at their feet.

A Colin grabbed it.

E Barbindar tried to pull it away from him.

A Barbindar tried to pull it away from him.

E They began to fight.

A They began to fight.

E Thorny brambles had ripped Barbindar's leg. "Ouch!" she screamed.

A Colin ran off.

E Freeing herself from the brambles, Barbindar chased after him.

A As they ran,

E the undergrowth became thicker. Rain began to fall.

A Colin looked back and saw Barbindar was struggling.

E He didn't care.

A He didn't care. He ran on.

E Then the ground gave way beneath him. "Help!" he cried. He had fallen into a deep pit. In the dark it seemed bottomless.

A Barbindar heard his cries and smiled.

E The ground shook beneath her.

A "Help me!" Colin called, slipping down the pit.

E There was something so frightened in his voice, Barbindar hurried over, despite her fears.

A "You're all right!" she answered. "There is a path to your left."

E As she spoke the rain eased off.

A At last Collin made his way to the top.

E He and Barbindar hugged with relief.

A "Here," he said, handing her the diamond, "take it."

E "Throw it away," she told him.

A "Throw it away," she told him.

E Collin threw it into the gaping dark pit.

A Collin threw it into the gaping dark pit.

E Hand in hand, they walked home.

2 & 3 No set response.

Storyboard
No set response.

Description: pages 32 & 33
Through work done on adjectives, pupils will be familiar with the nature of descriptive writing. These two pieces approach the subject from different angles. In *Aliens over Morpeth* the descriptions are a straight word picture of the aliens. In *Time Traveller holidays*, however, adjectives are used in a more coloured subjective way. They are designed not merely to describe, but to persuade. This leads in to the whole area of language use.

Answers
Aliens over Morpeth
1 Drawing should include: G2; round shape, trailing, silvery feelers with eye and nose at end

of each. ● T3; enormous, multi-coloured, jelly-like. Might be in perspex container. ● ZZ20; long and thin with shiny metalic skin, head a great coil, information ticks from head on thin, foil-like streamers.

2 G2: globular ● delicate ● peculiar ● sensitive ● small

T3: squidgy ● peculiar ● large ● gelatinous

ZZ20: hard ● intelligent ● peculiar ● linear

3 G2 desert: sand, dust ● T3 Antarctic: icy, slippery, freezing ● ZZ20 Pacific: water, salt, corrosion

4 No set response.

Time Traveller holidays
1 Adjectives include: legendary, titanic, huge, monster, terrifying, luxury, amazing, exciting, modern, hot

2 & 3 No set response.

Atmosphere: pages 34 & 35
In the first of these two pieces, an atmosphere has been described - in this case the brashness and vitality of the *Notting Hill Carnival*. In the form of a newspaper article, it seeks to capture some of the spirit of the event.

In *Macbeth* the atmosphere has been directly evoked - the darkness, fog, desolation of the moor and the presence of the weird sisters creating a sinister and suspenseful force.

Answers
Notting Hill Carnival
1 vibrant ● exciting ● noisy ● fun ● friendly

2 gaudy, bright and colourful ● bizarre, surprising and unusual

3 First held in 1965 ● biggest carnival in Europe ● lasts for two days ● covers 7km of streets ● 2 million visitors ● free

4 No set response

Macbeth
1 Few, thin ill-grown trees ● hard, sharp, boulders and stones ● fog blotting out the feeble moon ● wind ripped a raggedy hole ● figures in sickly moonlight

2 No set response.

3 It seemed they had risen from the ground. ● They looked as if they were waiting for something. ● "All hail Macbeth, next king of Scotland!" (They can see into the future.) ● With a spine-chilling laugh, the strange women disappeared.

Interpretation: pages 36 & 37
Our brains are constantly interpreting information of all kinds. How we choose to interpret the information flooding in, will very much depend on many factors such as age, sex and cultural experience.

Interpretation, therefore, is necessarily

subjective. The two exercises here are both, in a sense open ended. Clearly the Van Eyck painting is a wedding scene (chosen in part because many school libraries will contain a reproduction), but if, using the information available, a pupil can make a good alternative case as to what the picture represents - that alternative needs to be accepted!

Answers
The dark room
No set response.

Arnolfini
1 B
2 No set response.
3 Man is taller ● looking straight at viewer (woman's eyes are downcast) ● he seems to be signalling to the viewer ● he holds the woman's hand. Woman is passive, downcast eyes, head bent, side-on stance, hands held out to man.

Tone: pages 38 & 39

Every expression - written, verbal or non-verbal - has its particular register, or tone. This may be flat, serious, frivolous etc.

The richest man in the world seeks to make the point that the tone of a story is separable from meaning - its tone is light/comic, but its intention is serious. *Fire drill* looks at a variety of tone - four members of a family reacting to the same situation in different ways. Since tone is often conveyed as much by the way words are spoken (calm, depressed, excited etc.), as well as body language, it is suggested pupils work this scene as a play.

Answers
The richest man in the world
1 Funny
2 Serious
3 Richest man in the world ● Millions of them (cheques). ● ... give all his money away ● non-stop writing for two solid days ● Your parrots can have it (house)
4 & 5 No set response.

Fire drill
1 Paula: calm, serious ● Mum: excited, hysterical ● Bernie: jokey, insensitive ● Sandra: insensitive, complaining
2 Mature ● competent ● cool headed ● helpful ● concerned ● aware of people
3 No set response.

Mood: pages 40 & 41

Necessarily, mood is close to atmosphere, but in these exercises a distinction is drawn between internal and external experience. Atmosphere deals with the external, the mood pieces with an inner response.

Answers
Paintbox music
1 & 2 No set response.
On the beach
1 happy ● excited ● exuberant
2 Verse 2: trapped, helpless, prisoner, sleepy, immobile ● Verse 3: exhilarated, ecstatic ● Verse 4: weary, tired
3 Verse 1: morning ● Verse 2: midday ● Verse 3: afternoon
4 Verbs: am, leap, pounded, pummelled, tossed, turned, scream ● Adjectives: mad, crazy, freezing, crashing, raw ● Nouns: waves, surf, delight ● Predominance of verbs creates pace ● words are short and make poetry fast and energetic ● lack of full stops and commas keeps movement going, no interruptions.

Language use: pages 42 & 43

Children will already be aware that language use varies with circumstance - the language they use with their friends in the playground is (hopefully) different from the way they address the Head etc.

A day in the life investigates the variety of ways written language can be used to report the same event.

The magic bag is more an exercise in creative writing, encouraging pupils to explore the ways careful choice of word can expand their work - making it both more expressive and more informative.

Answers
A day in the life
1 C ● **2** E ● **3** A ● **4** D ● **5** B
No set response.

The magic bag
1 More expressive adjectives give reader extra information.
2 Altered verbs are: jumped, snorted, rummaged, extracted, hurled, transformed, roared, dragging. They show the woman's energetic and positive nature.
3 No set response.

Fact and opinion: pages 44 & 45

Being able to distinguish fact from opinion is one sign of a sophisticated reader, since it depends on being able to pick up often quite slight clues from the text. These exercises test the pupil's judgement.

Answers
Henry VII
1 F ● **2** F ● **3** F ● **4** F ● **5** O ● **6** O ● **7** F ● **8** O ● **9** O ● **10** F ● **11** O ● **12** F

Pirates

Inaccuracies include: Fortunately, piracy no longer exists • Pirates were always men • They often made their enemies walk the plank. • Most accurate information about pirates comes from novels, plays and films.

Bias and accuracy: pages 46 & 47

Even confident adult readers may often forget that what one reads is not necessarily definitive and impartial. Every writer brings to his or her work a collection of prejudices and preconceptions, often without being aware of them. These two exercises present different responses to a series of events, encouraging the pupil to examine why each character takes the view they do.

Answers
Cramer-on-Sea
Alan Mugimbi • Steve Norris • Jed Vaughan • Sally Zimmerman • Sarah Vaughan • Jess Vaughan • Michael Zimmerman

Vikings
1 C • D • A • B • E
2 Ranghild: life is tough, needs booty • Brenden Lamefoot: miserable, hates captivity • Prof Petersson: could be biased because he is Scandanavian • Brother Anselm: hates vikings for robbing church and killing • Harald the Brave: justifying his actions.
3 Because monks were only recorders theirs was only source of information to survive, bias was perpetuated.
4 **Good**: tough and brave, excellent builders and seamen, great craftsmen, loved poetry and song, democratic, supported each other. **Bad**: stole, murdered, kept slaves, frightened people.

Inference and deduction: pages 48 & 49

Comprehension activities can well be likened to the detective genre - pupils being asked a metaphorical "whodunit?" by their text

Like fictional detectives who on the hunt, sometimes have to draw disparate pieces of evidence together to make a convincing case, so pupils/readers are generally asked to gather evidence from a text. Judgements continually have to be made about such things as character, setting and language use etc.

Clearly, such judgements may in part be based on instinct, but still have to be backed up with reference to fact, as presented in the text. As in any detective work, deduction - the linking together of one piece of evidence to another to form a coherent argument - plays a great part. These two exercises help test those powers.

Answers
Camulodunum dig
1 Statues: religious but not Christian •

worshipped more than one god **Gold coins**: wealthy **Melted glass**: wealthy • comfortable • house burned **Jewellery**: wealthy **Pottery**: wealthy • sophisticated **Celtic sword and spear**: fighting had taken place • defence necessary **Broken swords**: as above **Mosaic and mural blackened**: wealthy • sophisticated • house burned
2 One answer from many possibilities: Roman house attacked then destroyed by fire. People were slain or escaped.
3 One answer from many possibilities: Owner of house might have been old soldier with collection of weapons. House may have burnt down due to spread of cooking fire.
4 No set response.

Computer game
1 & 2 No set response.

Cause and effect: pages 50 & 51

See Actions: Cause and effect

Answers
Rain
1 **C=Cause E=Effect**
C When warm air meets cold air,
E condensation takes place.
C The vapour "condenses",
E turning back into droplets of water.
C because warm air from cooking and baths hits cold window panes,
E you will often see condensation on windows.
C As soon as warm air meets cold,
E droplets of water form.
C the sun heats water (in puddles, ponds and lakes etc.),
E creating water vapour.
C Then, because warm air rises,
E the vapour is carried into the air.
C When warm air meets cold air,
E the vapour condenses into droplets, forming clouds.
C because they become too heavy,
E The drops fall as rain
2 Open ended but diagram might include:

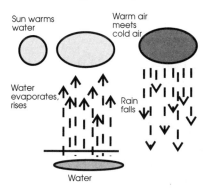

3 evaporation

Skin!
1 C=Cause E=Effect
C When you get too hot,
E blood vessels in your skin open wider
C when you exercise
E you go red.
C The air cools the blood near the surface,
E helping you to lose heat.
C When you're too hot,
E sweat is released through pores (tiny holes) in your skin.
C the sweat cools down in the air,
E so helping your body to cool.
C When the body is too cold,
E the muscles controlling hair tighten up.
C the muscles controlling hair tighten up.
E This makes your body hair stand up.
C air can become trapped between the standing hairs,
E helping to keep the animals warm.
C When the sun is very strong,
E your body produces a dye called melanin.
C your body produces a dye called melanin.
E This makes your skin darker,
C This makes your skin darker,
E helping protect it from the sun's harmful rays.
2 To protect skin you could: use sun block cream, avoid hot midday sun, wear protective clothing including hat and T-shirt.

Predicting: pages 52 & 53

At some point, in some way, in almost any sustained text, the question will be asked "What happens next?" Certainly, the need to answer this question drives most narratives.

Prediction, therefore, is an intrinsic reading skill, the ability to predict forward necessarily depending on an understanding of what has gone before, in terms of character, situation etc.

"Mystic Marge" is intended mainly to set pupils thinking about prediction and the future - and the variability of outcome. "The clay pot" requires a more informed response, and will show an understanding of the given information, as will an ability to continue the story in a consistent, plausible way.

Answers
Mystic Marge
1 travel • football • Prime Minister • drink • moon
2-4 No set response.

The clay pot
Several variations make sense including:
A, J, E, P • C, K, N, P • L, F, B, M • I, H, G, M • H, O, D, M

Identifying problems and solutions: pages 54 & 55

No reader comes to a text empty. We always bring with us to a piece of writing our preferences and prejudices (including, "I don't want to read this").

Children spend their lives solving problems, formal (can you subtract 24 from 267?) and informal (can I untie this knot in my shoelace?).

These two exercises tap into those problem solving skills. *Etti's Quest* is "closed" in that one problem has to be matched with a specific solution. *Sonu's problem* is open ended. It would be interesting to see the range of answers to his problem!

Answers
Etti's quest
D, B, A, C
No set response.

Sonu's problem
1 "Sticking to the rules" is incorrect.
2 No set response.
3 Reasons for Sonu to play: Sonu was desperately needed by his local football team, Traversham United. • He was their captain, leading goal scorer • easily the team's best player. • With Sonu's help, Traversham had won their way through to the Farrow League Cup Final. • he did not want to let his team down. • He knew his friends depended on him.
Reasons for Sonu to go on training weekend: the company had spotted his leadership potential • business course was a fast track to promotion. • By the age of twenty five he could be running a Darrant company anywhere in the world. • He found that prospect exciting.
4 One possible solution is for Sonu to approach Darrant and discuss his dilemma. As captain of his team he is getting leadership practise, which they should encourage. Local publicity of his involvement would be good for Darrant, particularly if Traversham win the cup. He could go on a later course.